Soft skills of tomorrow: preparing for the future of work

Copyright © 2024 Reginaldo Osnildo
All rights reserved.

PRESENTATION

INTRODUCTION TO THE SOFT SKILLS OF THE FUTURE

ADAPTABILITY AND FLEXIBILITY

CRITICAL THINKING AND PROBLEM SOLVING

CRIATIVITY AND INNOVATION

EMOTIONAL INTELLIGENCE

COLLABORATION AND TEAMWORK

EFFECTIVE COMMUNICATION

LEADERSHIP AND PEOPLE MANAGEMENT

CONTINUOUS LEARNING AND PERSONAL DEVELOPMENT

TIME MANAGEMENT AND PRODUCTIVITY

PROFESSIONAL ETHICS AND SOCIAL RESPONSIBILITY

NEGOTIATION CAPACITY

EMPATHY AND INTERPERSONAL RELATIONSHIPS

CULTURAL AWARENESS AND DIVERSITY

MINDFULNESS AND WELL-BEING

DATA-BASED DECISION MAKING

DIGITAL SKILLS

SUSTAINABILITY AND ECOLOGICAL CONSCIOUSNESS

CHANGE MANAGEMENT

STRATEGIC NETWORKING

RESILIENCE

SELF-MANAGEMENT

PERSUASION AND INFLUENCE

FEEDBACK AND CONSTRUCTIVE SELF-CRITICISM

INTEGRATING THE SOFT SKILLS OF THE FUTURE

REGINALDO OSNILDO

PRESENTATION

Welcome to the beginning of a transformative journey that will prepare you for the dynamic professional landscape that awaits us: " **Soft skills of tomorrow: preparing for the future of work** ". This book is an invitation for you, whether you are a student eager to take your first steps into the professional world or an experienced professional looking to adapt to new market demands, to delve into the skills most valued in the future of work.

We live in an era of accelerated change, where technology advances by leaps and bounds, transforming not only the way we live, but also the way we work. In this scenario, technical skills are essential, but it is the soft skills – those interpersonal and personal skills – that will determine who stands out and who is left behind. This book has been carefully crafted to provide you with in-depth insights into the soft skills needed to successfully navigate this new work environment.

Through the pages of this book, I will share my insights into how these core competencies have evolved and how you can develop them effectively. From adaptability and flexibility to leadership and people management, through to the importance of mental and physical well-being in the workplace, each chapter has been designed not only to synthesize existing knowledge, but also to enrich it with practical insights that will facilitate your learning and development journey.

You will find that by focusing on growing these skills, you can not only improve your employability, but also your professional effectiveness and job satisfaction. Throughout the book, you will be constantly reminded that developing these skills is an investment in your career and, most importantly, in yourself.

Each chapter is designed to be self-contained, providing a comprehensive understanding of each skill, along with practical strategies for developing them. But it's not just about learning; It's about applying this knowledge in your daily professional and personal life. Therefore, at the end of each chapter, I invite you to reflect on how these skills manifest in your life and how you can take concrete steps to improve them.

By embarking on this journey with us, you will take an important step towards preparing for the future of work. A future that values not just what you know, but who you are as a person and as a professional. Are you ready to get started? So, turn the page and enter the world of "Soft skills of tomorrow". The next chapter awaits you with valuable insights into the growing importance of soft skills in the job market of the future. Together, we'll explore how these skills will become your greatest allies in building a successful and meaningful career.

Yours sincerely

Reginaldo Osnildo

INTRODUCTION TO THE SOFT SKILLS OF THE FUTURE

As we move towards an increasingly unpredictable and technologically advanced future, the job market landscape is transforming at an unprecedented rate. In this chapter, you will discover why soft skills, or interpersonal skills, are becoming increasingly valued by employers and how they could be the key to not just surviving, but thriving in the future of work.

THE RISE OF SOFT SKILLS

Historically, technical skills were seen as the main factor in employability and professional success. However, as machines and artificial intelligence begin to take over technical and repetitive tasks, unique human skills are coming to the fore. The ability to adapt, think critically, innovate and collaborate are now more valued than ever. Studies and research from leading organizations such as the World Economic Forum consistently highlight soft skills as fundamental to the future of work.

WHY DO SOFT SKILLS MATTER?

You may wonder, "Why exactly are soft skills so important?" The answer is multifaceted. First, soft skills make it easier to adapt to changing work environments, allowing you to successfully navigate new challenges and technologies. Second, they are crucial for building solid professional relationships, whether with colleagues, clients or managers, fostering collaborative and productive work environments. Furthermore, soft skills improve leadership skills, encouraging motivation and innovation in teams.

DEVELOPING YOUR SOFT SKILLS

The good news is that, unlike many technical skills, soft skills can be developed regardless of your educational background or professional experience. Throughout this book, we will explore methods and practices for strengthening these essential skills. From reflection and self-awareness to deliberate practice and constructive feedback, you'll discover effective strategies for becoming a more adaptable, innovative, and collaborative professional.

TO THINK ABOUT

As you progress through this chapter, I invite you to reflect on the following questions: How have soft skills played a role in your career or education so far? What interpersonal skills do you believe are your strengths and which ones would you like to develop further?

This chapter is just the beginning of your journey to understand and improve the skills that will shape the future of work. As you dive into the following pages, you will gain valuable insights into each of the essential soft skills and learn practical strategies for cultivating them.

ADAPTABILITY AND FLEXIBILITY

As you prepare to turn the page, look forward to the next chapter, where we explore the importance of adaptability and flexibility. In this ever-changing world, the ability to quickly adjust to new environments and work situations is essential. Let's discover together how you can develop this crucial skill to confidently face the challenges that the future holds. Get ready to embark on a journey towards becoming a more resilient and versatile professional.

ADAPTABILITY AND FLEXIBILITY

In a world where the only constant is change, your ability to adapt and be flexible is not just a desirable skill; it is an absolute necessity. In this chapter, you will explore the essence of adaptability and flexibility in the modern workplace, and how these skills can be your greatest asset in an ever-evolving job market.

UNDERSTANDING ADAPTABILITY AND FLEXIBILITY

Adaptability refers to your ability to quickly adjust to new conditions, challenges, and work environments. It's the ability to "sail the waves" of changes without losing focus on your goals. Flexibility is complementary, relating to your willingness to change plans, strategies and behaviors in response to the changing needs of your work environment.

Together, these attributes allow you to view uncertainty and change not as obstacles, but as opportunities for growth and learning. In a world where technological transformations and disruptive innovations constantly redefine the parameters of professional success, being adaptable and flexible means always staying ahead.

WHY ARE THEY ESSENTIAL?

In a work environment that values innovation and speed, adaptability and flexibility are more than just useful skills; they are strategic imperatives. They allow you to:

- Approach unknown challenges with a problem-solving mindset rather than resistance.

- Maintain professional relevance by adjusting to new technologies and work methods.

- Collaborate effectively across a diversity of teams and projects, adjusting to different dynamics and expectations.

- Lead with confidence in uncertain situations, guiding your team through change with a positive and proactive outlook.

CULTIVATING ADAPTABILITY AND FLEXIBILITY

Developing adaptability and flexibility requires conscious practice and reflection. Here are some strategies to help you cultivate these skills:

- **Embrace change:** See change as an opportunity for growth. Challenge yourself to step out of your comfort zone regularly to become more comfortable with the unknown.

- **Develop a growth mindset:** Believe in your ability to learn and improve. View mistakes and failures as valuable lessons rather than obstacles.

- **Practice flexibility of thinking:** Train yourself to think about alternatives and possibilities. When faced with a problem, try to identify several potential solutions.

- **Stay informed:** Stay up to date on your industry trends and technological innovations. This will help you anticipate changes and adapt to them more quickly.

- **Cultivate resilience:** Develop your ability to bounce back from setbacks. View them as temporary steps on your path to success.

TO THINK ABOUT

As you progress through this chapter, reflect on situations in your professional or personal life where adaptability and flexibility were crucial to your success. How did you react to these changes? What did you learn from them?

This chapter is an invitation for you to embrace change, not just as an inevitable aspect of life, but as an opportunity to grow and thrive in any work environment. Adaptability and flexibility are not just about surviving change; it's about flourishing because of them.

CRITICAL THINKING AND PROBLEM SOLVING

As you prepare to turn the page, anticipate the next chapter, which will take you deep into the world of critical thinking and problem solving. You will discover how to develop the ability to analyze information effectively, think independently and find innovative solutions to the complex challenges of the modern workplace. Get ready to strengthen your mind with tools that will transform obstacles into stepping stones to your success.

CRITICAL THINKING AND PROBLEM SOLVING

In a world where information is abundant and complex situations are common, critical thinking and problem solving emerge as indispensable skills. This chapter is dedicated to exploring how you can develop these skills, enabling you to not only better understand the world around you, but also make informed decisions and find creative solutions to the challenges you face.

THE POWER OF CRITICAL THINKING

Critical thinking is the ability to analyze information and arguments objectively and rationally, identifying assumptions, evaluating evidence, and discerning valid conclusions from invalid ones. In essence, it is a way of thinking that questions everything, rather than accepting statements at first glance. In the workplace, critical thinking allows you to approach problems systematically, avoid common reasoning errors, and make decisions based on deep, well-founded analysis.

THE ART OF PROBLEM SOLVING

Problem solving is a direct application of critical thinking. It consists of the ability to face a challenge or an unwanted situation and work systematically to find an effective solution. In a professional context, this means being able to identify problems, explore possible solutions, evaluate alternatives and implement the most appropriate one. This skill is especially valued in dynamic work environments, where the ability to respond quickly and innovatively can be the difference between success and failure.

DEVELOPING CRITICAL THINKING AND PROBLEM-SOLVING SKILLS

Here are some strategies to strengthen your critical thinking and problem-solving skills:

- **Question assumptions:** Develop the habit of questioning assumptions, both yours and those of others. This can reveal new perspectives and possibilities.

- **Analyze information:** Practice analyzing information from various sources. Learn to identify biases, recognize patterns, and draw meaningful conclusions.

- **Engage in constructive discussions:** Participate in debates and discussions that challenge your thinking. Exposure to different points of view can improve your ability to argue and analyze.

- **Solve problems creatively:** See each problem as an opportunity to innovate. Explore alternative solutions and don't be afraid to experiment.

- **Learn from experience:** Reflect on the solutions you have implemented, both successful and failed. Every experience is a valuable lesson.

TO THINK ABOUT

As you progress through this chapter, reflect on situations in which critical thinking or problem solving were critical to your success. How did you approach these situations? What could you have done differently?

This chapter is not just a guide to thinking more effectively; is an invitation to become an innovative problem solver and confident decision maker. By cultivating critical thinking and problem-solving skills, you'll equip yourself with powerful tools to meet the challenges of the modern workplace and beyond.

CRIATIVITY AND INNOVATION

As you prepare to explore the next chapter, know that we will dive into the heart of innovation: creativity. Let's discover together how to unleash your creative potential, transforming ideas into innovative solutions that not only solve problems, but also open up new paths and opportunities. Prepare to be inspired and be inspired as we explore how creativity can be cultivated, nurtured and applied in all facets of your professional life.

CRIATIVITY AND INNOVATION

In a rapidly changing world, creativity and innovation are more than desirable skills; are essential for success and sustainability in the workplace of the future. In this chapter, we'll explore how you can unlock and nurture your creativity, turning it into innovation that not only solves problems, but also breaks new ground and creates unimaginable opportunities.

UNDERSTANDING CREATIVITY AND INNOVATION

Creativity is the ability to think of new ideas and concepts that are original and useful. It is the spark that ignites the fire of innovation. Innovation, in turn, is the practical application of these creative ideas to produce new and improved solutions, products or methods. Together, creativity and innovation form the engine that drives progress and development in all spheres of human activity, especially in the workplace.

WHY ARE THEY IMPORTANT?

Creativity and innovation are crucial because they enable organizations and individuals to adapt and thrive in markets and environments that are constantly changing. They are the key to solving complex problems, improving processes, developing new products or services and creating competitive advantage. In a professional setting, creative and innovative people are highly valued because they can see beyond the status quo, imagining possibilities that others cannot perceive.

UNLOCKING YOUR CREATIVITY

Here are some strategies to help you unleash and cultivate your creativity:

- **Conducive environment:** Create a physical and mental space that encourages experimentation and exploration. An environment free of judgment and open to new ideas is essential.

- **Diversify your experiences:** Expose yourself to

new experiences, cultures, and knowledge. Diversity of experiences enriches your mind and fuels your creativity.

- **Time to incubate:** Give yourself permission to daydream. The best ideas often come when we're not trying to force them.

- **Rapid prototyping:** Don't be afraid to fail. Quickly prototype your ideas, test them, learn from the results, and adjust as needed.

- **Collaboration:** Exchange ideas with other people. Collaboration can be a powerful tool for stimulating creativity and developing innovative solutions.

TO THINK ABOUT

As you progress through this chapter, think about the times when you felt most creative. What stimulated this creativity? Additionally, consider a recent situation where a creative approach could have been beneficial. How can you apply what you learned here to approach future challenges more creatively?

This chapter serves as a reminder that creativity and innovation are skills that everyone has and can develop. With practice, patience and the right mindset, you can turn your creative ideas into innovations that make a difference.

EMOTIONAL INTELLIGENCE

As you prepare to move forward, the next chapter will guide you through the world of emotional intelligence. You will discover how the ability to understand and manage your emotions and those of others can significantly improve communication, collaboration and leadership. Get ready to explore how emotional intelligence can be your most powerful ally in building strong professional relationships and achieving lasting success.

EMOTIONAL INTELLIGENCE

Emotional intelligence, a vital skill in today's and tomorrow's professional world, is the ability to recognize, understand and manage your own emotions as well as the emotions of others. In this chapter, we'll dive into the essence of emotional intelligence and discover how it can transform your professional effectiveness, your relationships at work, and your personal satisfaction.

UNDERSTANDING EMOTIONAL INTELLIGENCE

Emotional intelligence (EI) involves five key components: self-awareness, self-management, social awareness, relationship management, and empathy. Together, they form the foundation for effective communication, rational decision-making, inspirational leadership, and strong collaboration and negotiation skills. In the workplace, EI allows you to successfully navigate complex social situations, resolve conflicts constructively, and lead with empathy and understanding.

WHY IS EMOTIONAL INTELLIGENCE IMPORTANT?

In a world where automation and artificial intelligence are becoming increasingly prevalent, unique human skills like EI become increasingly valuable. The ability to connect on an emotional level with colleagues and clients can differentiate an average professional from an extraordinary one. Furthermore, emotional intelligence is key to creating a positive work environment where trust, mutual respect and collaboration flourish.

DEVELOPING YOUR EMOTIONAL INTELLIGENCE

Here are some strategies to strengthen your emotional intelligence:

- **Practice self-awareness:** Take time to reflect on your emotions and the causes behind them. Keeping a journal can be a useful tool for this practice.

- **Manage your emotions:** Learn emotional control techniques, such as deep breathing, to stay calm in stressful situations.

- **Develop empathy:** Try to put yourself in others' shoes to understand their points of view and emotions. This can significantly improve your interactions and communications.

- **Improve your social skills:** Practice active listening and assertive communication. Show genuine interest in the people around you and their concerns.

- **Cultivate positive relationships:** Invest time and energy to build and maintain healthy relationships at work. Be proactive in offering support and encouragement to others.

TO THINK ABOUT

As you explore this chapter, reflect on times when emotional intelligence has played a role in your professional life. How did self-management or empathy influence the outcomes of these situations? Consider areas where you could improve your EI and how this could impact your career.

Emotional intelligence is not only an essential skill for professional success; it is also fundamental to personal well-being and building meaningful relationships. By dedicating yourself to developing your EI, you are investing not only in your career, but also in your quality of life.

COLLABORATION AND TEAMWORK

As you prepare to advance, the next chapter will lead you to better understand collaboration and teamwork. You will discover how, regardless of your role, contributing effectively to a group can lead to exceptional results, promote innovation and create a positive work environment. Get ready to explore the keys to successful teamwork and how your emotional intelligence can enrich your contribution to any team.

COLLABORATION AND TEAMWORK

In today's dynamic workplace, collaboration and teamwork are not only beneficial; are indispensable. This chapter will guide you through the importance of building and maintaining strong teams, and how your contribution can catalyze collective success. Let's dive into strategies that can help you become a valuable team member and effective collaborator, regardless of your role or industry.

THE ESSENCE OF COLLABORATION AND TEAMWORK

Teamwork is the practice of working collectively to achieve a common goal, while collaboration involves sharing knowledge, learning and efforts to create something new or solve complex problems. Both are founded on effective communication, mutual trust, and respect, creating an environment where innovation and efficiency can flourish.

WHY ARE THEY CRUCIAL?

In an increasingly connected world, the ability to work well with others is more than a necessity - it's a requirement. Complex projects and ambitious goals often require a diversity of skills, perspectives and experiences that no single individual can possess. Furthermore, a collaborative work environment promotes a sense of belonging and engagement, which are crucial for talent retention and job satisfaction.

BUILDING COLLABORATION AND TEAMWORK SKILLS

To stand out in a collaborative environment, consider the following strategies:

- **Communicate effectively:** Practice active listening and clear communication. Make sure your ideas and feedback are understood and, conversely, strive to understand others' points of view.

- **Promote trust and respect:** Be trustworthy, keep your promises, and show respect for the ideas and contributions of others. A work environment where people feel valued is conducive to collaboration.

- Be adaptable: Be open to changes and new ideas. The ability to adapt and accept the contributions of others is crucial to successful teamwork.

- Encourage diversity of thought: Value the different perspectives and skills each member brings to the team. Diversity can be a powerful source of innovation and creative solutions.

- Develop emotional intelligence: Use your emotional intelligence to navigate and mediate conflicts, and to build strong relationships within the team.

TO THINK ABOUT

As you progress through this chapter, reflect on the teams you have been a part of. What worked well? Where were there challenges? How can you apply the lessons learned from these experiences to improve your collaboration and contribution to teamwork in the future?

Teamwork and collaboration are not only fundamental to professional success; they also enrich our work experience, making it more meaningful and satisfying. By investing in these skills, you not only become a valuable asset to your team, but you also cultivate a positive and productive work environment.

EFFECTIVE COMMUNICATION

As we move forward, the next chapter will explore effective communication, a cornerstone of both collaboration and teamwork. You will learn about the nuances of verbal and non-verbal communication, how to articulate your ideas clearly and listen in a way that strengthens relationships within your team. Get ready to unlock communication secrets that can transform the way you interact in the workplace.

EFFECTIVE COMMUNICATION

Communication is the art of transmitting information, ideas and emotions in a clear and understandable way. In the workplace, the effectiveness with which we communicate can significantly influence the success of our professional relationships, the productivity of our teams and, ultimately, the results of our projects. This chapter is dedicated to exploring the fundamentals of effective communication and how you can improve your communication skills to become a more effective collaborator and a more inspiring leader.

THE IMPORTANCE OF EFFECTIVE COMMUNICATION

Effective communication is essential for productive collaboration, conflict resolution and building a positive work environment. It allows not only the exchange of information, but also the building of relationships, the establishment of trust and the promotion of mutual understanding. Without it, misunderstandings and conflicts can arise, compromising team harmony and work efficiency.

PRINCIPLES OF EFFECTIVE COMMUNICATION

To communicate effectively, it is crucial to understand and practice the following principles:

- **Clarity and conciseness:** Be clear about the message you want to convey and avoid unnecessary details that could confuse the receiver.

- **Active listening:** Communication is a two-way street. Listen carefully, show interest in what the other person is saying and confirm your understanding.

- **Empathy:** Try to see things from the other person's point of view. Empathetic communication can help create a deeper connection and minimize conflict.

- **Constructive feedback:** Learn how to give and receive feedback in a way that promotes growth and improvement rather than causing resentment.

- **Audience Fit:** Tailor your message and communication style to your audience to ensure your message is received as intended.

DEVELOPING EFFECTIVE COMMUNICATION SKILLS

Improving your communication skills takes practice and reflection. Here are some tips to improve your ability to communicate effectively:

- **Practice self-awareness:** Be aware of how your words, tone of voice, and body language affect others.

- **Develop your listening skills:** Ask open-ended questions, paraphrase what was said to ensure understanding and avoid interrupting while the other person is speaking.

- **Learn to read body language:** Nonverbal communication can reveal a lot about the interlocutor's feelings and reactions.

- **Train assertiveness:** Learn to express your ideas and needs clearly and directly, respecting the opinions and needs of others.

- **Get feedback:** Ask for feedback on your communication skills and use it to develop yourself.

TO THINK ABOUT

As you progress through this chapter, think about situations where effective communication was crucial to success or where miscommunication caused problems. How can you apply the principles and strategies discussed here to improve your future interactions?

Effective communication is a powerful tool that can open doors to professional opportunities, improve relationships and facilitate team success. By investing in developing your communication skills, you put yourself on the path to achieving your professional and personal goals.

LEADERSHIP AND PEOPLE MANAGEMENT

As we move forward, the next chapter will explore leadership and people management. You will discover how to use your effective communication skills to inspire, motivate and guide your team towards success. Get ready to dive into the qualities of an effective leader and how you can cultivate them on your professional journey.

LEADERSHIP AND PEOPLE MANAGEMENT

Leadership transcends mere task management; is the art of inspiring and motivating people to achieve common goals with enthusiasm and commitment. This chapter reveals the secrets of effective leadership and how people management skills can positively transform a team's dynamics and results. As we explore these skills, you'll discover how to become the leader your team admires, respects, and is willing to follow.

UNDERSTANDING LEADERSHIP AND PEOPLE MANAGEMENT

Leadership is influence. It's about shaping and sharing a clear vision, setting goals and inspiring others to work together to achieve them. Effective leadership involves understanding the needs and motivations of each team member, promoting a positive work environment and encouraging professional and personal development.

People management, in turn, refers to the practices and skills necessary to effectively manage the performance and development of a team. This includes effective communication, delegation, feedback and recognition, as well as resolving conflict and promoting teamwork.

WHY ARE THEY CRUCIAL?

Effective leaders are able to turn an organization's vision into reality, creating a culture that promotes excellence, innovation and collaboration. They are essential for:

- Inspire and motivate the team.
- Navigate changes and challenges.
- Resolve conflicts and promote harmony.
- Develop the skills and capabilities of team members.
- Achieve organizational objectives and goals.

DEVELOPING YOUR LEADERSHIP AND MANAGEMENT SKILLS

To cultivate effective leadership and people management, consider the following strategies:

- **Be a role model:** Demonstrate the qualities you want to see in your team. Integrity, work ethic and passion are contagious.

- **Communicate clearly:** Use your effective communication skills to share visions, expectations and feedback in a clear and inspiring way.

- **Build strong relationships:** Take time to get to know your team. Understanding your aspirations, challenges and motivations can help you personalize your leadership approach.

- **Empower your team:** Delegate responsibilities, provide the necessary resources and trust your team to make decisions. This increases autonomy and engagement.

- **Promote professional development:** Encourage and facilitate opportunities for learning and growth. An effective leader cares about developing their team as much as achieving goals.

TO THINK ABOUT

As you explore this chapter, think about the leaders who have influenced your life. What qualities did they possess? How can you incorporate these qualities into your own leadership style? Also reflect on how you can improve your team management to promote a more productive and positive environment.

Leadership is a journey of constant learning and adaptation. By striving to improve your leadership and people management skills, you will not only achieve your organizational goals but also contribute significantly to the growth and satisfaction of your team.

CONTINUOUS LEARNING AND PERSONAL DEVELOPMENT

As you progress, prepare for the next chapter, which focuses on the importance of continuous learning and personal development. In this ever-changing world, adapting and continually growing is essential not only for professional success, but also for personal satisfaction. Discover how to cultivate a growth mindset that will keep you ahead of the game, no matter what challenges the future may bring.

CONTINUOUS LEARNING AND PERSONAL DEVELOPMENT

In a rapidly evolving world, the ability to continually learn and develop personally is not just a competitive advantage; it is a necessity. This chapter explores the importance of continuous learning and personal development, providing insights and strategies for cultivating a growth mindset. By embracing the journey of continuous learning, you prepare yourself not only to face the challenges of the future, but also to seize its opportunities.

UNDERSTANDING CONTINUOUS LEARNING AND PERSONAL DEVELOPMENT

Continuous learning is the process of acquiring new skills and knowledge throughout life, both for personal and professional reasons. Personal development, closely linked, is the conscious improvement of oneself, including aspects such as skills, talents and potential. Together, these concepts represent a commitment to personal and professional growth, adapting and evolving in response to changes and challenges.

WHY ARE THEY CRUCIAL?

Continuous learning and personal development are fundamental to:

- Stay relevant in an ever-changing job market.

- Improve employability, adaptability and innovation capacity.

- Increase self-efficacy, confidence and personal satisfaction.

- Stimulate creativity and the ability to solve complex problems.

DEVELOPING A GROWTH MENTALITY

To embrace continuous learning and personal development, a growth mindset is essential. Here are some strategies for growing it:

- **Accept challenges:** See challenges as opportunities to grow and learn, rather than insurmountable obstacles.

- **Persist in the face of difficulties:** Understand that effort and perseverance are fundamental parts of the learning and growth process.

- **Learn from feedback:** View feedback, even when negative, as a valuable opportunity for personal development.

- **Be inspired by the successes of others:** Instead of feeling envious, let the successes of others inspire you to achieve your own goals.

- **Be open to change:** Embrace change as a constant and see it as a chance to learn new things.

TOOLS AND RESOURCES FOR CONTINUOUS LEARNING

With the vast array of resources available today, learning has never been more accessible. Consider:

- Online courses and webinars on platforms such as Coursera, Udemy or Khan Academy.

- Podcasts and educational videos covering a wide range of topics.

- Books and articles in areas of interest or skill development.

- Networking networks and study groups for collaborative learning.

TO THINK ABOUT

As you progress through this chapter, reflect on the areas in which you want to grow. What skills would you like to develop or improve? How can you integrate continuous learning into your daily routine?

Committing to continuous learning and personal development is committing to your evolution as an individual and professional. By embracing this journey, you will not only achieve your goals but also discover new horizons to explore.

TIME MANAGEMENT AND PRODUCTIVITY

As we move forward, the next chapter will focus on a key component to personal and professional success: time management and productivity. You will learn effective strategies for organizing your time, prioritizing tasks and maximizing your efficiency. Get ready to transform how you approach your daily life, better balancing your responsibilities and finding more time for what really matters.

TIME MANAGEMENT AND PRODUCTIVITY

Effective time management and productivity are essential for success in any sphere of life, especially in a world where distractions are always within reach and the pressure to accomplish more in less time never ceases. This chapter offers practical strategies to help you manage your time effectively, increase your productivity, and achieve a healthy work-life balance.

UNDERSTANDING TIME MANAGEMENT AND PRODUCTIVITY

Time management is the process of planning and controlling how you spend the hours of your day to optimize your efficiency and productivity. Productivity, in turn, refers to how effectively you can complete tasks and achieve goals. Good time management allows you to work smarter – not harder – so you accomplish more in less time, even when time is short and pressures are high.

WHY ARE THEY IMPORTANT?

Effective time management and productivity are crucial because:

- Maximize your efficiency and effectiveness, allowing you to reach your goals faster.

- Reduce stress by minimizing last-minute rush and missed deadlines.

- They improve the quality of your work, as you can dedicate adequate time to each task.

- Help you achieve a work-life balance, ensuring you have time for the things you value most.

STRATEGIES TO IMPROVE TIME MANAGEMENT AND PRODUCTIVITY

- **Set clear priorities:** Identify your most important and urgent tasks and tackle them first. Use the Eisenhower principle to categorize tasks into urgent/important, important/non-urgent, urgent/not important, and non-urgent/not important.

- **Create a plan or schedule:** At the beginning of each day or week, make a plan of what tasks need to be completed and allocate specific time for each of them.

- **Avoid procrastination:** Use techniques such as the Pomodoro Technique to stay focused on tasks for defined periods, followed by brief breaks.

- **Delegate tasks:** Recognize when other people can do a task better or faster and delegate whenever possible.

- **Say no:** Learn to turn down tasks or commitments that don't align with your priorities or main goals.

- **Use time management tools:** Apps and digital tools can help you track your time, set reminders, and organize your tasks efficiently.

TO THINK ABOUT

As you explore this chapter, reflect on your own time management and productivity practices. What are the biggest challenges you face? What strategies can you start implementing to overcome these challenges?

Effective time management and increased productivity are not just about getting more done in less time, but about doing what matters most efficiently, allowing you to live a fuller, more balanced life.

PROFESSIONAL ETHICS AND SOCIAL RESPONSIBILITY

As we move forward, the next chapter will address professional ethics and social responsibility, two fundamental pillars for building a solid career and contributing positively to society. You will discover the importance of adopting ethical practices at work and how social responsibility can enrich your professional and personal life. Get ready to explore how to integrate these core values into your growth and development journey.

PROFESSIONAL ETHICS AND SOCIAL RESPONSIBILITY

In an increasingly connected and conscious world, professional ethics and social responsibility emerge as fundamental elements for any successful career. This chapter addresses the importance of acting with integrity in the workplace and contributing positively to society. Let's explore how you can incorporate these essential principles into your professional journey, making a lasting impact in both your personal and collective spheres.

UNDERSTANDING PROFESSIONAL ETHICS AND SOCIAL RESPONSIBILITY

Professional ethics refers to the principles and values that guide the behavior of individuals in a work environment. This includes honesty, integrity, transparency and fairness. Social responsibility concerns the commitment of individuals and companies to contribute to a fairer and more sustainable society, recognizing the impact of their actions on common well-being.

WHY ARE THEY IMPORTANT?

Adopting an ethical and socially responsible stance is crucial because:

- Builds trust and credibility with colleagues, customers and the community.

- Promotes a positive work environment and a culture of mutual respect.

- Contributes to the sustainable development and well-being of society.

- Differentiates individuals and organizations in an increasingly conscious market.

INTEGRATING ETHICS AND SOCIAL RESPONSIBILITY INTO YOUR CAREER

- **Be an example:** Demonstrate ethical conduct in all your actions and decisions. Being a model of integrity inspires others to follow the same path.

- **Promote fair practices:** Whether in hiring, treating colleagues or conducting business, ensure that your actions are always fair and transparent.

- **Contribute to the community:** Engage in volunteer activities or initiatives that benefit the local community or greater causes. Even small actions can have a big impact.

- **Stand up for what is right:** When you come across unethical or harmful practices, speak up. The courage to defend ethical principles is fundamental to promoting change.

- **Educate yourself and others:** Stay informed about ethical and social issues relevant to your profession and share this knowledge with your colleagues.

TO THINK ABOUT

As you progress through this chapter, think about how professional ethics and social responsibility apply in your field of work. Are there areas where you can do more to promote ethical conduct or contribute to the well-being of society?

Incorporating professional ethics and social responsibility into your career not only enriches your professional life, but also contributes to a fairer and more sustainable society. By adopting these principles, you not only achieve personal success, but also become part of a larger movement that aims to create a better future for everyone.

NEGOTIATION CAPACITY

As we move forward, the next chapter will explore negotiation skills, an essential skill in any professional context. Learning to negotiate effectively can not only help you achieve better results in agreements and projects, but also help you resolve conflicts constructively. Get ready to discover negotiation techniques that will enable you to create win-win solutions and strengthen your professional relationships.

NEGOTIATION CAPACITY

Trading is an art and a science. It is the process of discussing and reaching a mutual agreement, where all parties involved find common ground. This chapter is dedicated to improving your negotiation skills, an essential skill that can define the success of your professional interactions and projects. The ability to negotiate effectively can help resolve conflicts, establish productive partnerships and ensure the best possible results for all parties involved.

UNDERSTANDING NEGOTIATION CAPACITY

Negotiation involves communication, exchanging information and using strategies to reach a satisfactory agreement. Efficiency in negotiation requires understanding one's own needs and objectives, as well as those of the other party, creating solutions that benefit everyone involved.

BECAUSE IT'S IMPORTANT?

The ability to negotiate is crucial because:

- Facilitates beneficial agreements, avoiding conflicts and misunderstandings.

- Improves professional relationships through mutual respect and understanding.

- Contributes to the success of common projects and objectives.

- Elevates your reputation as a valued collaborator and trusted partner.

DEVELOPING YOUR NEGOTIATION SKILLS

To become an effective negotiator, consider these strategies:

- **Prepare adequately:** Before entering into a negotiation, collect as much information as possible about the other party and the context. Know your goals, limits, and alternatives.

- **Actively listen:** The ability to listen carefully and understand the other party's point of view is crucial. This can reveal underlying interests and pave the way for creative solutions.

- **Communicate clearly:** Be clear and concise in your communication. Avoid misunderstandings by expressing your needs and goals directly.

- **Emphasize win-win:** Look for solutions that benefit all parties. Successful negotiations are those in which everyone is satisfied.

- **Know when to back down:** Recognizing that not all negotiations will result in an agreement is important. Knowing when to walk away can save valuable resources and preserve relationships.

TO THINK ABOUT

As you explore this chapter, reflect on your past trading experiences. What strategies worked? Where can you improve? Think about how you can apply these lessons learned in future negotiations to achieve even better results.

Negotiation is a vital skill that transcends the professional environment, also benefiting personal interactions. Mastering the art of negotiation allows you not only to achieve goals effectively, but also to build and maintain solid and productive relationships.

EMPATHY AND INTERPERSONAL RELATIONSHIPS

The next chapter will dive into the importance of empathy and developing strong interpersonal skills. These are keys to building trusting and collaborative relationships in any work environment. Get ready to learn how empathy can significantly improve your communication and the effectiveness of your professional interactions.

EMPATHY AND INTERPERSONAL RELATIONSHIPS

Empathy, the ability to understand and share another person's feelings, is a fundamental pillar for developing strong and meaningful interpersonal relationships in the workplace. This chapter is dedicated to exploring empathy and the importance of interpersonal relationships, highlighting how these skills can improve your communication, collaboration and contribute to a more cohesive and productive work environment.

UNDERSTANDING EMPATHY AND INTERPERSONAL RELATIONSHIPS

Empathy goes beyond simple sympathy; It is the ability to put yourself in someone else's shoes, understanding their perspectives and emotions in a deep and genuine way. Interpersonal relationships refer to the connections and interactions we maintain with others, which are fundamental to creating a collaborative and supportive work environment.

WHY ARE THEY IMPORTANT?

Empathy and strong interpersonal skills are crucial because:

- They facilitate effective communication, allowing a better understanding of the needs and expectations of others.

- Promote a positive work environment, reducing conflicts and misunderstandings.

- Increase collaboration and team spirit, as members feel valued and understood.

- Contribute to effective leadership, allowing leaders to inspire and motivate their teams more effectively.

DEVELOPING EMPATHY AND INTERPERSONAL SKILLS

To strengthen your empathy and interpersonal skills, consider the following strategies:

- **Practice active listening:** Focus completely on what the other person is saying, acknowledging their feelings and perspectives without judgment.

- Show genuine interest: Show curiosity and interest in the experiences and emotions of others by asking open-ended questions that encourage expression.

- Communicate sensitively: Adapt your communication to the emotional needs of others, being careful with the language and tone used.

- Develop self-awareness: Reflect on your own emotions and reactions to better understand how they can affect your interactions with others.

- Be supportive: Offer support and understanding when others are facing challenges, showing that you value their well-being.

TO THINK ABOUT

As you progress through this chapter, think about times when empathy or lack thereof influenced your work relationships. How could you have improved these interactions? Identify opportunities to practice empathy and strengthen your interpersonal relationships in the future.

Empathy and interpersonal skills are not only essential for a harmonious work environment; they are vital to success in all areas of life. By developing these skills, you not only become a more effective professional, but also a more understanding and connected person.

CULTURAL AWARENESS AND DIVERSITY

The next chapter will cover cultural awareness and the importance of diversity in the workplace. The ability to understand, respect and value cultural differences can tremendously enrich the workplace, promoting innovation, creativity and a spirit of inclusion. Get ready to explore how you can contribute to a more diverse and inclusive workplace .

CULTURAL AWARENESS AND DIVERSITY

Cultural awareness and diversity are fundamental in today's globalized and multifaceted world. This chapter focuses on the importance of understanding, respecting and valuing cultural differences, as well as promoting inclusion in the workplace. We'll explore how cultural awareness can enrich collaboration, drive innovation, and contribute to a workspace where everyone feels valued and included.

UNDERSTANDING CULTURAL AWARENESS AND DIVERSITY

Cultural awareness refers to the ability to recognize and understand one's own and others' cultural beliefs, realizing how these influences shape perceptions, behaviors, and interactions. Diversity, in turn, encompasses a wide range of differences, including, but not limited to, race, ethnicity, gender, age, sexual orientation, ability and religion.

WHY ARE THEY IMPORTANT?

Promoting cultural awareness and diversity is crucial because:

- Enriches the work environment with a variety of perspectives and ideas, promoting creativity and innovation.

- Improves decision making and problem solving by incorporating a broader range of views and experiences.

- Builds stronger, more understanding relationships between colleagues, increasing collaboration and efficiency.

- Reflects positively on the image and values of the organization, attracting talent and clients from diverse backgrounds.

DEVELOPING CULTURAL AWARENESS AND PROMOTING DIVERSITY

To cultivate an inclusive and diverse work environment, consider the following strategies:

- **Educate yourself:** Actively seek to learn about different cultures, histories and experiences. This may include reading, attending workshops, or direct interactions with individuals from different backgrounds.

- **Listen and learn:** Be open to hearing the experiences of others without judgment, showing respect and empathy for their perspectives.

- **Foster an inclusive environment:** Implement policies and practices that promote equality and inclusion, such as diversity and inclusion training, mentoring and support for employee networks.

- **Celebrate diversity:** Recognize and celebrate cultural differences through events, festivities and recognition, valuing the richness that each individual brings to the work environment.

- **Advocate for inclusion:** Be an active ally to colleagues who face discrimination or exclusion, advocating for change and supporting equal opportunities for all.

TO THINK ABOUT

Reflect on how cultural awareness and diversity manifest in your current work environment. Are there areas where inclusion can be improved? How can you contribute to a more diverse and welcoming workspace ?

Embracing diversity and cultivating cultural awareness not only enriches the workplace, but also prepares organizations to operate successfully on a global stage. By promoting inclusion, you contribute to a world where the richness of human differences is celebrated and valued.

MINDFULNESS AND WELL-BEING

As we move forward, the next chapter will explore the importance of mindfulness and well-being in the workplace. Practicing mindfulness can significantly improve your mental and physical health, your ability to concentrate, and your effectiveness at work. Get ready to discover how to integrate mindfulness practices into your daily routine to promote holistic well-being and a greater quality of life.

MINDFULNESS AND WELL-BEING

In the current era, marked by rapid changes and constant demands, the practice of mindfulness and the promotion of well-being have never been more important. This chapter is dedicated to exploring how incorporating mindfulness into your daily routine can improve your mental and physical health, your concentration, and, ultimately, your effectiveness at work and satisfaction in life.

UNDERSTANDING MINDFULNESS AND WELL-BEING

Mindfulness is the practice of being fully present and engaged in the current moment, aware of our thoughts, emotions, bodily sensations and environment, without judgment. Well-being refers to a state of health, happiness and prosperity where an individual is able to fulfill their potential, cope with the normal stresses of life, work productively and contribute to their community.

WHY ARE THEY IMPORTANT?

Practicing mindfulness and promoting well-being are crucial because:

- Reduce stress and anxiety, improving mental health.

- Increases the ability to concentrate and mental clarity, leading to greater productivity.

- Improve sleep quality and physical health.

- They enrich the quality of interpersonal relationships through greater empathy and patience.

- They encourage greater emotional resilience, enabling individuals to better deal with challenges and changes.

INTEGRATING MINDFULNESS AND WELL-BEING INTO YOUR ROUTINE

To cultivate mindfulness and promote your well-being, try integrating the following practices into your daily life:

- **Daily meditation:** Dedicate time every day to practice meditation, focusing on your breathing or bodily sensations to bring your attention to the present.

- **Breathing exercises:** Use conscious breathing techniques to center your mind and calm your body in times of stress.

- **Mindfulness in daily activities:** Practice being fully present in routine activities, such as eating, walking or bathing, observing all the sensations involved.

- **Digital disconnection:** Establish periods of the day to disconnect from electronic devices and social media, reducing excess stimuli.

- **Cultivate gratitude:** Keep a gratitude journal, writing down things you are grateful for every day, promoting a positive outlook on life.

TO THINK ABOUT

As you progress through this chapter, consider how practicing mindfulness could impact your professional and personal life. Are there areas of your life where you could benefit from greater mindfulness and well-being?

Incorporating mindfulness and promoting well-being not only enriches your life experience, but also improves your performance and satisfaction in the workplace. By adopting these practices, you open yourself up to a life of greater clarity, balance, and happiness.

DATA-BASED DECISION MAKING

Get ready to explore data-driven decision making in the next chapter. In this information-driven world, learning to interpret and use data effectively can transform your ability to make informed decisions, minimize risks and maximize results. Discover how to improve your analytical skills and become a more efficient and strategic decision maker.

DATA-BASED DECISION MAKING

In an environment increasingly dominated by vast amounts of information, the ability to make informed, data-driven decisions is more crucial than ever. This chapter focuses on the importance of data analysis in the decision-making process, offering insights into how you can improve your analytical skills to make more effective decisions, reduce risk, and drive the success of your initiatives.

UNDERSTANDING DATA-DRIVEN DECISION MAKING

Data-driven decision making involves using quantifiable information and analysis to guide choices and actions. This process requires the collection, analysis and interpretation of relevant data to evaluate options, predict outcomes and determine the best course of action.

BECAUSE IT'S IMPORTANT?

Taking a data-driven approach to decision-making is essential because:

- Improves decision accuracy by reducing uncertainty and personal bias.

- Facilitates trend forecasting and pattern recognition, enabling proactive responses to changes.

- Increases the efficiency and effectiveness of operations by focusing on informed strategies and actions.

- Strengthens confidence in decisions made, both individually and as a team.

DEVELOPING SKILLS FOR DATA-BASED DECISION MAKING

To become proficient in data-driven decision making, consider adopting the following practices:

- **Improve your analytical skills:** Invest in training or courses that teach you how to collect, analyze and interpret data effectively.

- **Use data analysis tools:** Familiarize yourself with software and analytical tools that can help organize, visualize and analyze data.

- **Cultivate data curiosity:** Develop a questioning mindset, always looking for data that can support or challenge your assumptions.

- **Learn from data:** Use historical data to understand past trends, errors and successes, applying these learnings to future decisions.

- **Promote data culture:** Encourage the use and appreciation of data as a basis for decisions in your team or organization.

TO THINK ABOUT

As you explore this chapter, think about situations where data-driven decision making could have significantly impacted results. How can you start integrating more data into your everyday decisions?

Data-driven decision making is a powerful skill that can transform how you approach problems and opportunities. By using data to light the way, you can make more confident and strategic decisions that will drive success in any endeavor.

DIGITAL SKILLS

The next chapter will address digital skills, essential in the information age in which we live. With technology continually advancing, staying up to date with the digital skills needed to effectively navigate the professional and personal world is imperative. Get ready to explore how you can develop and enhance your digital skills to stay relevant and competitive in today's job market.

DIGITAL SKILLS

Navigating the digital era competently is an undeniable necessity in the contemporary world, both for professional and personal development. This chapter focuses on the essential digital skills you need to stay relevant and effective in today's workplace, which is constantly evolving due to technological advancement.

UNDERSTANDING DIGITAL SKILLS

Digital skills cover a wide range of competencies, from the ability to effectively use digital tools and platforms to understanding more complex concepts such as data analysis and software development. They allow individuals to communicate, create, collaborate and solve problems in digital environments, fundamental to practically all areas of work today.

WHY ARE THEY IMPORTANT?

Digital skills are crucial because:

- They facilitate adaptation to new tools and technologies that are reshaping the work environment.

- Increase employability, as most jobs now require some level of digital competence.

- Enhance efficiency and productivity through task automation and process optimization.

- Support innovation and creativity, offering new ways to approach problems and create solutions.

DEVELOPING YOUR DIGITAL SKILLS

To improve your digital skills, consider adopting the following strategies:

- **Join online courses:** Take advantage of the wide range of courses available online to learn new digital skills, from programming to graphic design and digital marketing.

- **Practice regularly:** Familiarity with digital tools and platforms comes with practice. Take time to explore and use different types of software.

- **Stay up to date:** The field of technology is always evolving. Stay informed about the latest trends and digital tools by reading specialized publications and attending webinars and workshops.

- **Explore digital problem solving:** Develop your own projects or participate in hackathons and other events that challenge your digital and creative skills.

- **Build a tech network:** Connecting with technology professionals can provide valuable insights and collaborative learning opportunities.

TO THINK ABOUT

As you explore this chapter, consider which digital skills are most relevant to your career or personal goals. How can you begin to integrate developing these skills into your daily routine?

Mastering digital skills is critical to successfully navigating today's world. By investing in the continuous development of these skills, you not only ensure your relevance in the job market, but also open doors to endless opportunities for growth and innovation.

SUSTAINABILITY AND ECOLOGICAL CONSCIOUSNESS

The next chapter will address the importance of sustainability and ecological awareness, highlighting how sustainable practices can be integrated into the workplace and beyond. As the world faces unprecedented environmental challenges, it is essential for professionals in all fields to adopt a greener stance. Get ready to explore strategies that not only benefit the planet, but can also lead to greater efficiency and innovation in your professional activities.

SUSTAINABILITY AND ECOLOGICAL CONSCIOUSNESS

In a world facing unprecedented environmental challenges, sustainability and ecological awareness emerge as imperatives not only for the survival of the planet, but also for the future of work. This chapter highlights the importance of integrating sustainable practices in the workplace and beyond, encouraging reflection on how individual and collective actions can have a lasting positive impact on the environment.

UNDERSTANDING SUSTAINABILITY AND ECOLOGICAL CONSCIOUSNESS

Sustainability refers to the ability to meet the needs of the present without compromising the ability of future generations to meet their own needs. Ecological awareness, on the other hand, concerns understanding the impact of our actions on the natural world and adopting a way of life that minimizes this impact.

WHY ARE THEY IMPORTANT?

Adopting a sustainable approach and ecological awareness is crucial because:

- Helps preserve vital natural resources and biodiversity.

- Contributes to reducing pollution and greenhouse gas emissions.

- Supports social and economic equity by promoting fair and sustainable practices.

- Can improve operational efficiency and reduce costs in the long term.

- Strengthens the image and brand of companies that are seen as responsible and environmentally conscious.

INTEGRATING SUSTAINABILITY INTO THE WORK ENVIRONMENT

To promote sustainability and ecological awareness in your professional activities, consider the following strategies:

- **Adopt green office practices:** Minimize paper use, recycle, use energy efficiently and choose suppliers that also prioritize sustainability.

- **Promote sustainable mobility:** Encourage the use of public transport, bicycles or carpooling to get to work.

- **Promote environmental awareness:** Educate yourself and colleagues about environmental issues and how everyday actions can contribute to sustainability.

- **Embed sustainability into business operations:** Evaluate supply chain, production processes and consumption practices to identify and implement more sustainable approaches.

- **Support green initiatives:** Participate in or organize reforestation campaigns, cleaning public spaces and other activities that promote the well-being of the environment.

TO THINK ABOUT

Reflecting on this chapter, think about how you and your organization currently impact the environment. What changes can you make to adopt a more sustainable lifestyle and work practices?

Adopting sustainable practices is not just an ethical responsibility; It is an opportunity to lead by example, inspiring others to act for the common good. By incorporating sustainability and ecological awareness into your professional practices, you contribute to a greener and fairer future for everyone.

CHANGE MANAGEMENT

Get ready to explore change management in the workplace in the next chapter. In an ever-changing world, the ability to adapt and lead through change is more valuable than ever. Discover strategies to successfully navigate change, minimizing stress and maximizing both personal and organizational resilience.

CHANGE MANAGEMENT

In a world characterized by constant innovation and rapid change, the ability to manage and lead through change becomes indispensable for professionals at all levels. This chapter covers change management, emphasizing techniques and strategies to help you adapt, overcome resistance, and capitalize on the opportunities that change brings.

UNDERSTANDING CHANGE MANAGEMENT

Change management is the systematic process of transitioning individuals, teams and organizations from a current state to a desired future state. It involves using approaches and techniques to help people understand, accept and adopt changes in the workplace.

BECAUSE IT'S IMPORTANT?

Effective change management is crucial because:

- Facilitates adaptation to new policies, processes, technologies and ideas.

- Minimizes resistance to change, reducing stress and anxiety among employees.

- Improves communication and engagement, ensuring everyone is aligned with the future direction.

- Increases the likelihood of success of change initiatives, maximizing return on investment.

STRATEGIES FOR EFFECTIVE CHANGE MANAGEMENT

To successfully navigate through change, consider implementing the following strategies:

- **Communicate clearly and transparently:** Provide clear information about what is changing, why it is changing, and how the change will affect each person.

- **Engage and support stakeholders:** Include team members

in the change planning and implementation process. Offer support, like training and resources, to help them adapt.

- **Create a shared vision:** Develop and communicate a clear vision of the desired state after the change, highlighting the benefits for everyone involved.

- **Promote leadership by example:** Leaders and managers must embrace and model the changes they hope to see in their teams.

- **Monitor and adjust:** Track the progress of the change and be open to making adjustments based on feedback and results achieved.

TO THINK ABOUT

As you progress through this chapter, reflect on the changes you have experienced in your professional life. What strategies have been effective in helping you adapt? How can you apply these learnings to future transitions?

Change management is a vital component to success in an ever-evolving workplace. Mastering the skills needed to lead and manage change not only prepares you and your team for the future, but also opens doors to new opportunities and growth.

STRATEGIC NETWORKING

In the next chapter, we will explore the power of strategic networking. Building and maintaining a valuable professional network is not just about meeting more people; it's about building meaningful relationships that can support your career goals and personal development. Get ready to discover how to cultivate an effective and strategic networking network that can be a source of opportunities, knowledge and support.

STRATEGIC NETWORKING

Strategic networking is an essential skill in building a successful career and personal development. It's not just about increasing the number of contacts, but about establishing and nurturing meaningful relationships that are mutually beneficial. This chapter is dedicated to exploring how you can effectively build and maintain a valuable professional network, highlighting strategies for creating connections that support your career goals and growth.

UNDERSTANDING STRATEGIC NETWORKING

Strategic networking involves identifying and developing relationships with individuals within and outside your industry who can provide valuable insights, support, opportunities and resources. It's an intentional, targeted process that requires more than just exchanging business cards; it requires authenticity, reciprocity and long-term commitment.

BECAUSE IT'S IMPORTANT?

Effective strategic networking is crucial because:

- Opens doors to new career opportunities, partnerships and collaborations.

- Provides access to new knowledge, skills and industry insights.

- Expands your influence and visibility in the sector.

- Provides support through mentoring, advice and feedback.

- Contributes to personal growth through exposure to different perspectives and experiences.

STRATEGIES FOR EFFECTIVE STRATEGIC NETWORKING

To develop a strategic professional network, consider implementing the following strategies:

- **Define your networking goals:** Be clear about what you

hope to achieve through your networking. This will help identify the most relevant people and groups to connect with.

- **Be authentic:** Build relationships based on sincerity and genuine interest. The strongest connections are formed when there is a real exchange of value and mutual interest.

- **Offer value:** Before asking for help or advice, think about how you can offer value to others. This could include sharing knowledge, offering support or connecting people with similar interests.

- **Use social media and professional platforms:** Tools such as LinkedIn, Twitter and virtual events can be excellent ways to connect with professionals from different areas.

- **Stay in touch:** Effective networking requires maintenance. Have regular check-ins with your network, share relevant updates, and celebrate others' successes.

TO THINK ABOUT

As you progress through this chapter, think about the professional relationships you already have. How can you deepen these connections? What specific actions can you take to strategically and intentionally expand your network?

Strategic networking is an art that, when practiced effectively, can bring immeasurable benefits to your career and personal development. By investing time and energy into building a meaningful network, you lay a solid foundation for future success.

RESILIENCE

The next chapter will focus on resilience, the ability to recover quickly from difficulties and adversity. In a professional world full of challenges and uncertainties, resilience is not just desirable, it is essential. Get ready to explore how to strengthen your resilience, allowing you to face obstacles with determination and flexibility, transforming challenges into opportunities for growth.

RESILIENCE

Resilience is an essential quality in a professional environment characterized by constant challenges, changes and uncertainties. This chapter explores the concept of resilience, highlighting its importance and offering strategies for developing and strengthening this essential capacity, enabling you to face adversity with determination, adaptability, and a positive outlook.

UNDERSTANDING RESILIENCE

Resilience is the ability to quickly recover from difficulties, adapt to changes, overcome obstacles and resist pressure in adverse situations. It is a combination of emotional, mental and physical skills that allows a person to face challenges head on and emerge from them stronger and more prepared.

BECAUSE IT'S IMPORTANT?

Being resilient is crucial because:

- Makes it easier to manage stress and overcome setbacks.

- Contributes to personal growth by transforming challenges into learning opportunities.

- Improves the ability to deal with uncertainty and change.

- Promotes a positive attitude in the face of difficulties.

- Strengthens persistence and determination to achieve long-term goals.

STRATEGIES FOR DEVELOPING RESILIENCE

To cultivate and strengthen your resilience, consider the following practices:

- **Cultivate a growth mindset:** See challenges as opportunities to learn and grow, rather than insurmountable threats.

- **Develop support networks:** Build and maintain strong

relationships with colleagues, friends and family who can offer emotional and practical support.

- **Manage your emotions:** Learn techniques to understand and control your emotions, allowing you to face situations with greater clarity and calm.

- **Practice self-care:** Take care of your physical and mental health, including regular exercise, healthy eating, adequate sleep and mindfulness practices.

- **Set realistic goals:** Set clear, achievable goals, and celebrate small successes on the way to bigger goals.

- **Adopt a positive outlook:** Try to maintain an optimistic attitude, focusing on what you can control and seeking to find the positive side of situations.

TO THINK ABOUT

As you read this chapter, think about situations in which your resilience was put to the test. How did you react? Which strategies were effective and which could be improved?

Developing resilience is an ongoing process that requires awareness, practice and commitment. By strengthening your resilience, you not only prepare yourself to face challenges more effectively, but you also pave the way for continued growth and success, both personally and professionally.

SELF-MANAGEMENT

Get ready to explore the next crucial topic: self-management. The ability to manage yourself, including your emotions, time and resources, is fundamental to achieving success and satisfaction in both professional and personal life. The next chapter will provide valuable insights and techniques to enhance your self-management, helping you navigate more efficiently and purposefully toward your goals.

SELF-MANAGEMENT

Self-management is an essential skill that permeates all aspects of life, enabling us to manage our emotions, behaviors, time and resources effectively. This chapter addresses the importance of self-management for achieving success and satisfaction, both professionally and personally, and offers strategies for improving it.

UNDERSTANDING SELF-MANAGEMENT

Self-management involves a series of skills and practices that allow a person to direct their own behavior and well-being in a productive and healthy way. This includes setting goals, planning and prioritizing tasks, managing time effectively, regulating emotions, and boosting self-motivation.

BECAUSE IT'S IMPORTANT?

Effective self-management is crucial because:

- Increases productivity and efficiency by optimizing how time and resources are used.

- Improves the ability to deal with stress and adversity, promoting resilience.

- Facilitates the achievement of personal and professional goals.

- Contributes to healthier relationships and effective communication, by managing your own emotions and reactions.

STRATEGIES TO IMPROVE SELF-MANAGEMENT

To strengthen your self-management skills, consider the following approaches:

- **Set clear goals:** Establish specific, measurable, achievable, relevant and time-bound (SMART) objectives to direct your efforts effectively.

- **Develop action plans:** For each goal, create a detailed plan for how you intend to achieve it, including specific steps, deadlines, and resources needed.

- **Prioritize tasks:** Use time management tools and techniques, such as task lists and the Eisenhower matrix, to identify and focus on the most important activities.

- **Cultivate discipline:** Develop routines and habits that support your goals and objectives, remaining firm in their execution, even in the face of challenges.

- **Manage your emotions:** Learn emotional intelligence techniques to recognize, understand and regulate your emotions, especially in pressure or stressful situations.

- **Stay motivated:** Identify what motivates you and use these factors to boost your energy and commitment to your goals.

TO THINK ABOUT

Reflect on how you currently manage yourself in the different areas of your life. Which aspects of self-management have you already mastered and which ones need to be improved?
Self-management is the basis for a successful and balanced professional and personal life. By improving your self-management skills, you gain greater control over your journey, allowing you to confidently navigate toward your goals.

PERSUASION AND INFLUENCE

The next chapter will unpack the skills of persuasion and influence, showing how they are crucial for leading, negotiating and promoting effective change. The ability to persuade and influence others can open doors and create opportunities, both in your personal and professional lives. Get ready to explore techniques and strategies to develop your ability to persuade and exert a positive influence around you.

PERSUASION AND INFLUENCE

The art of persuasion and the power of influence are fundamental tools in any professional's repertoire. This chapter explores how the ability to persuade and positively influence others can open doors, create opportunities, and facilitate effective leadership, negotiation, and implementation of change. Here, you will learn techniques and strategies to develop your ability to impact decisions and behaviors, maximizing your potential for success.

UNDERSTANDING PERSUASION AND INFLUENCE

Persuasion is the process of convincing someone to do something or accept an idea through communication, without the use of force or coercion. Influence, on the other hand, refers to the ability to affect the character, development, or behavior of someone or something. Together, these skills allow you to guide interactions toward mutually beneficial outcomes.

WHY ARE THEY IMPORTANT?

Persuading and influencing are crucial because:

- Facilitate effective leadership, allowing you to inspire and motivate your team.

- They help in negotiating favorable agreements and resolving conflicts.

- Allow the promotion and defense of ideas, projects and innovations.

- Contribute to building solid professional relationships and contact networks.

DEVELOPING PERSUASION AND INFLUENCE SKILLS

To improve your persuasion and influencing skills, consider the following practices:

- **Know your audience:** Understand the needs, wants and motivations of those you want to influence, adapting your approach as necessary.

- **Communicate with clarity and conviction:** Be clear in your message and deliver it with confidence to inspire confidence in others.

- **Establish credibility:** Build and maintain a reputation for reliability, competence and integrity.

- **Use reciprocity:** People tend to give back what they receive. Offer help, information or resources before asking for something in return.

- **Apply social proof:** Demonstrate that your ideas or proposals have the support or approval of others, especially respected individuals or groups.

- **Engage emotions:** In addition to presenting logical arguments and data, engage your audience's emotions. Personal stories, metaphors, and examples that stir feelings can be powerful.

- **Demonstrate empathy:** Show that you understand and value the perspectives and feelings of others. This can help reduce resistance and build trust.

- **Be flexible:** Be prepared to adjust your approach based on feedback and reactions from your audience. Flexibility demonstrates consideration and respect for others' points of view.

TO THINK ABOUT

Think about situations where you needed to persuade or influence someone. What strategies worked? What could you have done differently? Reflecting on these experiences can provide valuable insights to improve your persuasion and influencing skills.

Developing the ability to persuade and influence is an ongoing process that requires practice, reflection and adaptation. By improving these skills, you become more capable of leading effectively, driving positive change, and achieving your professional and personal goals.

FEEDBACK AND CONSTRUCTIVE SELF-CRITICISM

Moving forward, the next chapter will address the importance of feedback and constructive self-criticism. The ability to give, receive and apply feedback productively is essential for personal and professional growth. Furthermore, cultivating the capacity for critical self-evaluation allows you to identify areas for improvement and act proactively. Get ready to explore how these skills can be developed and applied to foster continuous development and excellence.

FEEDBACK AND CONSTRUCTIVE SELF-CRITICISM

Feedback and constructive self-criticism are essential tools for continuous growth and improvement in the professional and personal environment. This chapter explores the importance of giving and receiving feedback effectively, as well as practicing self-criticism in a productive way, aimed at personal development and skill improvement.

UNDERSTANDING FEEDBACK AND CONSTRUCTIVE SELF-CRITICISM

Feedback refers to information or criticism about someone's performance, intended to guide future improvements. Constructive self-criticism is the ability to critically evaluate one's performance, recognizing both successes and failures, and identifying areas for development.

WHY ARE THEY IMPORTANT?

- **Feedback:** Provides external perspectives on your performance, highlighting areas of strength and opportunities for growth.

- **Constructive self-criticism:** Encourages self-awareness and personal responsibility for ongoing development, allowing you to become your own mentor.

DEVELOPING THE PRACTICE OF FEEDBACK AND CONSTRUCTIVE SELF-CRITICISM

To fully benefit from feedback and constructive self-criticism, consider the following strategies:

- **Create an environment of openness:** Encourage an environment where feedback is viewed as a development tool, not personal criticism.

- **Be specific:** Both when giving and receiving feedback, be specific. Focusing on concrete examples makes feedback more understandable and applicable.

- **Focus on the behavior, not the person:** When giving feedback, focus on specific behaviors or actions that can be changed, avoiding character judgments.

- **Practice active listening:** When receiving feedback, listen carefully, ask questions to clarify, and don't rush to defend yourself.

- **Establish action plans:** Use feedback and self-criticism to develop specific action plans aimed at personal and professional improvement.

- **Keep a reflection journal:** Record reflections on your performance, feedback received, and progress toward your goals. This can help identify patterns and areas for continuous improvement.

TO THINK ABOUT

Consider recent times when you have received feedback. How did you react? Is there anything you could do differently to make better use of this learning opportunity? Likewise, think about how you approach self-criticism. Is it balanced and growth-oriented?

Mastering the art of feedback and constructive self-criticism is essential for any professional who aspires to growth and excellence. These practices not only promote personal and professional development, but also strengthen working relationships by fostering open communication and mutual support.

INTEGRATING THE SOFT SKILLS OF THE FUTURE

As we approach the end of this book, the next chapter will serve as a conclusion, revisiting the topics covered and reflecting on how to effectively integrate all of the soft skills discussed to prepare for a dynamic and constantly evolving professional future. Get ready to consolidate your learning and chart a path forward, equipped with the interpersonal and personal skills needed for success.

INTEGRATING THE SOFT SKILLS OF THE FUTURE

Throughout this book, we explore a wide range of essential soft skills that will prepare you to confidently face the future of work. From adaptability and critical thinking to leadership and change management, each chapter provided insights and strategies for developing the interpersonal and personal skills most valued in the modern professional world. This concluding chapter is intended to bring these concepts together, offering insight into how to effectively integrate these skills into your ongoing development journey.

REVIEW OF ESSENTIAL SOFT SKILLS

Each soft skill covered in this book contributes to a portfolio of skills that makes you not only a more capable professional, but also a more resilient, adaptable and effective person in any work environment. Remember that:

- **Adaptability and flexibility** are fundamental in an ever-changing world.

- **Critical thinking and problem solving** empower you to navigate complex challenges with clarity and innovation.

- **Creativity and innovation** open doors to new ideas and solutions.

- **Emotional intelligence** and **communication skills** strengthen your relationships and facilitate effective collaboration.

- **Leadership** inspires others to achieve common goals together.

- **Continuous learning** ensures you stay relevant and ahead of the changing curves.

INTEGRATING SOFT SKILLS INTO YOUR LIFE

Integrating these soft skills into your professional and personal life is not a one-time event, but an ongoing process of growth and adaptation. Here are some tips for incorporating these skills effectively:

- **Self-assessment:** Regularly take time to reflect on your current skills and areas for development. Utilize feedback from peers, mentors, and your own constructive self-criticism.

- **Set development goals:** Based on your self-assessment, establish clear goals for developing specific soft skills. Create detailed action plans with actionable steps.

- **Deliberate practice:** Dedicate time to practice new skills, whether through simulations, participation in workshops, or everyday challenges at work.

- **Seek feedback:** Stay open to feedback and see it as a valuable opportunity for continued growth.

- **Stay curious:** Be a lifelong learner, always seeking new information, skills and experiences.

LOOKING TO THE FUTURE

As you embark on your ongoing journey of personal and professional development, remember that soft skills are just as important as technical skills. They are the foundation upon which lasting success is built, especially in a world that values adaptability, innovation and collaboration. Equipped with the strategies and insights provided in this book, you are prepared to face the challenges of the future of work, turning every opportunity into success.

We encourage you to revisit the chapters in this book whenever you need guidance or inspiration, remembering that developing soft skills is an ongoing journey, enriched by each new experience and learning along the way.

As we turn the final page of this journey together, I sincerely hope that the learnings shared here have touched your heart and sparked new perspectives. If this book has brought you any value, I kindly ask that you take a few moments to leave a review on Amazon. Your words not only help me grow and hone my craft, but they also guide other readers in their quests for knowledge and inspiration. Your opinion is a valuable gift, both for me and for the community of readers looking for stories that transform. I sincerely thank you for sharing this journey with me and I hope we can meet again in the pages of a new adventure.

REGINALDO OSNILDO

Hello, I'm Reginaldo Osnildo, author and innovator in the fields of sales, technology, and communication strategies. My background spans from the academic setting, as a professor and researcher at the University of Southern Santa Catarina, to hands-on strategy development at the Catarinense Radio Group. With a PhD in sales narratives and digital convergence, and a Master's in storytelling and social imaginary, I offer my readers a unique blend of theory and practice. My aim is to deliver knowledge in a simple, practical, and didactic language, encouraging direct application in one's personal and professional life.

Yours sincerely

Reginaldo Osnildo

+55 48 991913865

reginaldoosnildo@gmail.com

www.ingramcontent.com/pod-product-compliance
Lightning Source LLC
Chambersburg PA
CBHW050327230526
45471CB00005B/2382